Contents

Foreword

My dear friend, Professor Stephen Inbanathan, has helpfully brought to our attention the wonderful insights of a much-neglected book of the Hebrew Bible, the prophecy of Habakkuk. Not only this, but he demonstrates very perceptively how Habakkuk fearlessly grapples with perhaps the most challenging issue of faith, the question of how it can be that the God of love can endure the presence of evil and suffering in the world he has created. This was a terrifying reality for Habakkuk himself, as Inbanathan explains in his clear and concise introduction to the historical situation which surrounded the prophet at that time, but he goes on carefully to make it clear that what Habakkuk learnt is important for our time also, since we, like the prophet, are living through an era of disquiet and trouble.

There have been two major strands of thinking about the problem of evil, or theodicy as it has come to be called. St Augustine wrote in his famous Confessions that, 'Free will is the cause of our doing evil and Thy just judgement is the cause of our having to suffer from its consequences.' Another early church writer,

Irenaeus, believed however that evil and suffering in the world were created by God in order that by undergoing those torments we would mature as Christians. It is surely correct to say that suffering can help us grow in character and spiritual maturity but it might seem to many of us that if Irenaeus is right then it was a very harsh way for God to teach us to become better human beings. Professor Inbanathan therefore decides to let Habakkuk speak for himself, for the prophet seems to arrive at a subtly different answer to the problem of evil from either of those proposed by Augustine or Irenaeus.

We are often taught that to appreciate the will of God we should listen to the innermost reaches of our own hearts but Professor Inbanathan also reminds us that the early Hebrews understood the role of the prophet as being one who sees, and indeed I Samuel Chapter 9 verse 9 tells us that, 'the one who is now called a prophet was formerly called a seer.' The prophet Habakkuk is therefore told by God that as well as listening he should also become a watch-man – looking at what was happening around him in order to see and understand what God's purposes were, for if he looked out for it he would see God penetrating every element of his day to day history. One of the great insights of the Hebrew people was that God acts in history to bring about the salvation of the world – what the theologians came to call 'Heilsgeschichte', which is German for 'salvation history'. And Habakkuk is a prime example of that tradition of interpreting Israel's history to perceive how within it God was fulfilling his purposes for his people. By drawing our attention to this approach Professor Inbanathan begins to unpack, line by line, what Habakkuk was seeing and learning and perceptively highlights for us how utterly rigorous with the truth this courageous prophet was. Habakkuk opens up to God his most anguished doubts and fears, holding nothing back, and setting out before his Lord both his terror at the prospect of an invasion of his country and laying bare his worry that God should allow this to happen, visiting disaster and suffering upon his people. Professor Inbanathan takes us carefully through the process which Habakkuk undergoes, helping us to see the extent of the problem with which the prophet struggled, on behalf of us all.

Perhaps it is because he is a specialist in advanced physics that Stephen Inbanathan is careful to work from what we see before us in the biblical text rather than overwrite it with our own presuppositions, and by doing so we begin to see that Habakkuk learns to appreciate that although his God never condones or glories in the actions of violent nations, God nevertheless takes those actions and transforms them in accordance with his own purposes towards the greater good of his righteousness. Thus he can say that with God all things – even the violence of the evil Babylonian empire – work together for good, and for our salvation, for God grasps hold of even the most evil action and makes good come of it. As I read this fascinating biblical exposition I could not help thinking of that penetrating verse from Psalm 85, 'Mercy and truth are met together; righteousness and peace have kissed each other,' for the professor has helped us to see how the honest truth of historical fact is, with God, shot through with mercy, and how God's righteousness or justice requires peace for its true glory to be manifest.

The problem of evil and suffering will forever challenge the believer, but Professor Inbanathan's exposition can remind us always to be lookers at the world's stark issues as well as listeners to the inner promptings of God if we are to present ourselves before our Lord with the integrity and faithful grace of the prophet Habakkuk

The Right Reverend Doctor Laurie Green, U.K

Acknowledgements

I would like to thank many people who helped me to bring this book.

First, I thank Rev.Dr.Bill Allen for his insights, observations and editorial contributions. I also thank his wife Cynthia for reading the manuscript carefully.

I thank Bishop Laurie Green for writing the foreword which brings out the content of the book in a very meaningful way.

To my wife Dr.Rani Rosaline for her constant support and love for me and for the greatest gifts Chrislyne and Christa, our children.

S.STEPHEN RAJKUMAR INBANATHAN
October 1, 2021

Chapter 1

Introduction

The book of Habakkuk is a theodicy; it addresses the problem of evil in the world. It raises and answers perennial questions about why God allows injustice to prevail throughout society. In view of a growing global pandemic of evil, how can people today believe in the existence and goodness of God? This brief prophecy records the intimate and intense personal relationship between Habakkuk and God. It is a testament to God's constant concern for the covenant community and to God's guidance of world history.

Historical Setting

Habakkuk lived during the seventh century before the birth of Christ. It was a period of national turmoil caused by systemic social injustice. To fully appreciate Habakkuk, it is absolutely essential to understand the backstory of God's covenant relationship with Abraham and his descendants. God promised to produce, protect and perpetuate the nation of Israel, the descendants of Abraham. Through Abraham's descendants, God further promised to establish an everlasting kingdom. Israel was originally established as a federation of tribes under God's guidance until they became a united kingdom under Saul, their first king. Israel remained united through the reigns of David and Solomon but upon the death of Solomon, a civil war divided Israel in two–Israel in the north and Judah in the south. A century before Habakkuk was born, in 721 B.C. the Assyrians conquered and captured the northern part of the nation–Israel–leaving only the people of Judah in the south as surviving heirs to God's covenant promises. The endurance of Israel's southern kingdom of Judah was the only remaining hope for future survival and final fulfillment of God's promise to establish justice on earth as it is in heaven.

Authorship

The author's name is also the title of the book. He identifies himself in the opening verse and again at the beginning of the third chapter. In both verses, he introduces himself as "Habakkuk", the prophet. This indicates that he was a professional prophet who may have served in the temple at Jerusalem. The literary style of the book reveals that Habakkuk was also a poet and liturgical priest. Rabbinical scholars refer to him as a musician and Levite because of the book's musical notation–found also in Psalms–and because the Levites were charged with providing musical accompaniment for the Jerusalem temple worship ceremonies. The meaning of his name may come from the Hebrew word "habaq" which means to embrace. It refers to somebody who hugs or clings. According to Martin Luther, this name is significant because Habakkuk embraced his people to comfort and uphold them.

Habakkuk bears the right name to his commission. For Habakkuk means to hug. He does so with his prophecy by hugging or embracing his people. He comforts them and takes them into his arms as one does with a crying child or adult. (Martin Luther's Prefix to the Prophet Habakkuk)

Alternatively, Jerome interpreted it to mean that Habakkuk embraced the problem of divine justice in the world, the book's central theme. Above all, Habakkuk embraced God.

Chapter 2

The prophecy that Habakkuk the prophet received

The prophecy that Habakkuk the prophet received. Habakkuk identifies his prophecy as a revelation received directly from God. It is not a message born of the prophet's own imagination; it is from God. The Hebrew word here translated as received is from a verbal root which means to see; it implies that Habakkuk may have received God's revelation in a visionary experience.

Habakkuk's First Question: How Can God Ignore Judah's Sin?

2 How long, Lord, must I call for help, but you do not listen? Or cry out to you "violence!" but you do not save?

3 Why do you make me look at injustice? Why do you tolerate wrongdoing? Destruction and violence are before me; there is strife, and conflict abounds.

4 Therefore the law is paralyzed and justice never prevails. The

wicked hem in the righteous so that justice is perverted.

Habakkuk's first problem is made perfectly clear by four Hebrew words that he selected to describe the social situation in Judah: violence, iniquity, oppression and destruction. As Habakkuk saw it, the nation of Judah was spiritually and morally bankrupt. Since sin ran rampant, injustice prevailed and prevented God's law from operating effectively. Habakkuk was troubled because God's covenant community was not behaving the way God prescribed. After witnessing deplorable behaviour throughout the city of Jerusalem, the prophet cried out to God in prayer: God, how can you tolerate all this evil? In your holy city, violence, injustice, oppression and destruction dominate - yet You appear to be doing nothing about it. Why do you make me look at it all? Habakkuk wanted God to bring judgement on evildoers and restore law and order to society. Similarly, people still pray, "Lord, why don't You reform our society and restore civility so that it will be safe to walk the streets again? Habakkuk courageously confronted God and earnestly pleaded for an explanation. Habakkuk took his questions about God directly to God.

God's Answer: Babylonians are God's Agent of Chastisement.

5 "Look at the nations and watch–and be utterly amazed. For I am going to do something in your days that you would not believe, even if you were told.

6 I am raising up the Babylonians, that ruthless and impetuous people, who sweep across the whole earth to seize dwellings not their own.

7 They are a feared and dreaded people; they are a law to themselves and promote their own honor.

8 Their horses are swifter than leopards, fiercer than wolves at dusk. Their cavalry gallops headlong; their horsemen come from afar.

9 They fly like an eagle swooping to devour; they all come intent on violence. Their hordes advance like a desert wind, and gather prisoners like sand.

10 They mock kings and scoff at rulers. They laugh at all fortified cities; by building earthen ramps, they capture them.

11 Then they sweep past like the wind and go on–guilty people, whose own strength is their god."

In answering Habakkuk, God throws the prophet's own words back at him. Whereas Habakkuk had complained that he was forced to look at unrestrained evil, God told him to look at the nations and watch. God was already at work behind the scenes of human history, guiding events to fulfill the divine purpose and plan. When Habakkuk learned what God was about to do, he became so bewildered that he could barely believe it. The reason for his astonishment lies in the historical fact that Babylonia was not yet widely known as a rising superpower. However by the end of Habakkuk's generation, in fulfillment of his prophecy,

Babylonia had conquered all rival kingdoms to become the dominant empire of the ancient near east. By revealing to Habakkuk the future dominance of Babylonia, God assured the prophet that everything happens under God's supervision and guidance. Since Habakkuk was evidently unfamiliar with the Babylonians, God provided him with a vivid vision of their cruel and ruthless ways. They will terrorize everyone and refuse to recognize or heed any law above themselves. God gives Habakkuk a glimpse of the Babylonian armed forces, likening them to ferocious leopards, ravenous wolves, vicious birds of prey swooping down to devour helpless victims, and a windstorm that sweeps up all the sand in its path. They ridicule rival rulers, taunt neighboring nations and make a mockery of enemy defenses by building ramps to scale walls and conquer cities. Habakkuk had complained about the violence that filled his nation and God would respond by visiting the violence of the Babylonians on Judah. Though the Babylonians were merely an agent of God's judgment on Judah, instead of acknowledging God, they gave credit to their own gods for their devastation and defeat of Jerusalem. God assures the prophet that the violent Babylonians will in turn also be punished. When nations exalt themselves and their military might above the one true and living God, they will not be held guiltless.

Habakkuk's Second Question: How can a Holy God Use the Evil Babylonians?

12 Lord, are you not from everlasting? My God, my Holy One, we will never die. You, Lord, have appointed them to execute judgement; you, my Rock, have ordained them to punish.

13 Your eyes are too pure to look on evil; You cannot tolerate wrongdoing. Why then, do you tolerate the treacherous? Why are You silent while the wicked swallow up those more righteous than themselves?

14 You have made people like the fish in the sea, like the sea creatures that have no ruler.

15 The wicked foe pulls all of them up with hooks, he catches them in his net, he gathers them up in his dragnet; and so he rejoices and is glad.

16 Therefore he sacrifices to his net and burns incense to his dragnet, for by his net he lives in luxury and enjoys choicest food.

17 Is he to keep on emptying his net, destroying nations without mercy?

With a rhetorical question, Habakkuk reminds himself that God is eternal, reassuring himself that God will preserve a righteous remnant from among the covenant community. God's eternity guarantees God's faithfulness. By reminding himself of God's eternity, Habakkuk declares his complete confidence in God's promise to preserve a remnant of those in Judah who have been declared righteous by faith. Moreover, because God is eternal, Habakkuk can confidently declare: My God, my Holy one, we will not die." By addressing God as my Holy One, Habakkuk appeals to the core characteristic of God's nature. Habakkuk now acknowledges that God has appointed the Babylonians to punish Judah. Nevertheless, Habakkuk cannot understand how the Holy One, who is too pure to look approvingly on evil, can collaborate with the oppressive and morally reprehensible Babylonians. Previously Habakkuk complained that God had not judged Judah for its sinfulness, and God assured Habakkuk that judgement was on its way. But when God revealed that the wicked Babylonians were to be the instrument of God's judgment against the relatively less sinful nation of Judah, Habakkuk was bewildered. He detected an apparent contradiction between the holiness and justice of God. How can a holy God employ an evil agent to execute divine justice? Habakkuk compares the Babylonians to fishermen and the people they conquer are like teams of fish that are caught in their nets. The nets symbolize the Babylonian military machine to which the idolatrous Babylonians sacrifice and offer worship. Habakkuk wondered how long God would allow the evil Babylonians to continue conquering nations with impunity. Moreover, he feared that once God let them loose to wreak havoc on humanity, there would be no one, including God, who would ever be able to stop them. On the one hand, the prophet maintained faith in God to preserve a righteous remnant from among the people of Judah but, on the other hand, Habakkuk's faith faltered, fearing that the Babylonians might annihilate the entire population of Judah. From the prophet's personal point of view, God's covenant promise to the patriarchs was in serious peril.

Chapter 3

Yahweh's Answer about Babylonia: God Controls all Nations According to Divine Purpose

1 I will stand at my watch and station myself on the ramparts; I will look to see what God will say to me, and what answer I am to give to this complaint.

Having gained renewed confidence in God, Habakkuk announces his resolve to fill the role of watchman, waiting in anticipation of God's message for the nation. Habbakuk uses the watchman as a figurative expression for his inward, spiritual preparation to be informed and enlightened by God. Just as the watchman on the wall waits patiently, watching for enemy advances, Habakkuk waits expectantly for a revelation and correction from God. Habakkuk has posed two questions; they are serious questions for which he earnestly desires an answer from God. How can You justify using an exceedingly evil empire to punish a much less corrupt nation like Judah, and how long will You permit the Babylonians to plunder and pillage the nations without consequence? These were not merely rhetorical questions disguised as accusations or criticisms. Habakkuk believed that God must have valid reasons for administering divine justice by the cruel Babylonians but he could not understand why God would bring judgement that way. Habakkuk was prepared to wait and watch for God's answer; he was ready to be both corrected and enlightened by God. Just as Habakkuk wanted God to chastise Judha for its sin, he was willing to be chastised himself by God's reply. The questions were Habakkuk's way of saying to God: I don't see the justice or logic in the way You are operating but I want to understand and appreciate the reasons so please change my outlook by explaining it all to me. He fully expected God to reply. *2* Then the Lord replied: "Write down the revelation and make it plain on tablets so that a herald may run with it. *3* For the revelation awaits an appointed time; it speaks of the end and will not prove false. Though it may seem to linger, wait for it; it will certainly come and will not delay."

God directed Habakkuk to record their conversation and publish it clearly for the enlightenment and encouragement of those who would read it in the future. The revelation was to be plain, preserved and perpetuated. The prophetic message was intended for a future time that no one, including Hababkkuk, had seen coming. Intended to refer specifically to the Babylonian invasion of Jerusalem, the prophecy was permanently committed to writing for the benefit of all future generations, including our own. God assured Habakkuk that the fulfillment of the prophecy he was about to receive would occur in the future so that all who read it may see how God guides world history according to divinely revealed principles of justice.

God's Indictment of Babylonia

4 "See the enemy is puffed up; his desires are not upright–but the righteous person will live by faith– The principles of God's righteous governance of the world are here plainly revealed to the prophet. God rewards faith and punishes pride. Faith expresses itself in a life of righteous living in conformity to God's prescribed way of behavior. Pride reveals itself in arrogance, conceit and rejection of God. Habakkuk was troubled that God would use the exceedingly evil nation of Babylonia to punish the relatively less sinful nation of Judah. Here, God assures Habakkuk that the Babylonians' haughty pride has not gone unnoticed and will not go unpunished. In sharp distinction to the proud are those whom God declares righteous. Pride is a primary source of conceit whereas faith is the foundation of righteousness. God characterizes the righteous person in the midst of a description of the proud person to dramatize the difference between the two. Pride places confidence in the self whereas faith looks beyond the self to trust in God. Habakkuk can rest assured that God will justly govern the world of people and nations in accordance with their relationship to God and God's righteous ways. In the face of an imminent Babylonian invasion, Habakkuk need not question God any longer; he needs only to remain faithful and trust God to do what is right. By clinging to God, the righteous person enjoys spiritual life; by rejecting God,

wicked people live in spiritual death. Biblical scholars claim that this is the single most central and significant verse in the entire Bible. According to one rabbinic tradition, it summarizes all 613 laws revealed by God to Moses. According to Christian interpretive tradition, this verse was the biblical catalyst that ignited the Protestant Reformation. Martin Luther had been studying Paul's exposition of this verse in Romans 1:17 when he wrote: There I began to understand that the righteousness of God is that by which the righteous lives by a gift of God, namely by faith. And this is the meaning: the righteousness of God is revealed by the gospel, namely, the passive righteousness with which merciful God justifies us by faith... Here I felt I was altogether born again and had entered paradise itself through open gates. There an entirely new face of the entire Scripture showed itself to me.

This pivotal verse from Habakkuk is quoted verbatim three times in the New Testament. Paul quoted it in his letter to the Romans to teach them that the righteous person is justified in God's sight by faith alone; the justified person meets with God's approval only by faith in God. Paul had quoted the same verse in his letter to the church at Galatia (Galatians 3:11) to instruct them how to live a spiritual life. Rather than receiving spiritual life as a result of obeying the law of Moses, the righteous person is empowered to live a spiritual life by faith in God. The author of the New Testament letter to the Hebrews (10:38) also cited this verse to teach salvation by faith. It is by faith that God will reward the righteous with eternal life. Those who understand Habakkuk 2:4 grasp the gospel of God and what it means to live a spiritual life. It is the key to understanding the book of Habakkuk and the main message of the entire Bible.

5 Indeed, presumption betrays him; he is arrogant and never at rest. Because he is as greedy as the grave and like death is never satisfied, he gathers to himself all the nations and takes captive all the peoples."

The righteous principles of God's governance presented in verse 4 are now applied to the unrighteous Babylonians. The proud Babylonians betray themselves with their own presumption. Death and the grave are personified as hungry monsters and likened to prideful people who are never content or fulfilled. Like death itself, they are incessantly driven by their own insatiable appetite for power over people. Selfish ambition engenders ungodly desires toward everyone and everything. Just as death devours life so the Babylonians pillage and plunder everything in their path. But their selfish desires will become the cause of their own demise. God will allow the proud Babylonians to doom themselves with their own depraved, degenerate and decadent desires.

Woe Against Aggression

There are five foreboding pronouncements against those who behave like Babylonia. Habakkuk presents the woeful warnings in the literary form of taunt songs as if they were addressed to the Babylonians by the nations they pillaged and plundered. Each of the five woes speaks to specific sins of the Babylonians.

6 "Will not all of them taunt him with ridicule and scorn, saying: 'Woe to him who piles up stolen goods and makes himself wealthy by extortion. How long must this go on?' 7 Will not your creditors suddenly arise? Will they not wake up and make you tremble? Then you will become their prey. 8 Because you have plundered many nations, the peoples that are left will plunder

you. For you have shed human blood; you have destroyed land and cities and everyone in them."

Regarding the first woe, the Babylonians were notorious for taking what was not theirs. Moreover, they confiscated the bare necessities of life from those whom they conquered. The victims of this aggression cry out "How long?" as the invaders continue to take what does not belong to them. But God will not allow them to get away with it and announces judgement against Babylonia: "because you have looted many nations, all the remainder of the peoples will loot you because of human bloodshed and violence." As the Babylonians have done to others, so it will be done unto them.

Woe Against Evil Scheming

9 Woe to him who builds his house by unjust gain, setting his nest on high to escape the clutches of ruin! 10 You have plotted the ruin of many peoples, shaming your own house and forfeiting your life. 11 The stones of the wall will cry out, and the beams of the woodwork will echo it.

The second woe exposes Babylonia's sinful strategizing to acquire the wealth of others by violence and deceit. The passage alludes to the Babylonian building projects which were accomplished by means of the exploitation and oppression of conquered populations. The very stones and woodwork of the building projects will cry out against the Babylonians.

Woe Against Violence

12 Woe to him who builds a city with bloodshed and establishes a town by injustice! 13 Has not the Lord Almighty determined that the peoples labor is only fuel for the fire, that the

nations exhaust themselves for nothing. *14* For the earth will be filled with the knowledge of the glory of the Lord.

The passage calls further attention to the bloodshed and injustice by which the Babylonians built their empire. People of violence believe that might makes right but God abhors violence and condemns those who commit it. Woe to them who build a city based on violence and bloodshed. Habakkuk quotes from Isaiah to remind his readers that God is in complete control of all things to come. All other glory seekers like Babylonia will be silenced by God whose glory alone will fill the entire earth. The ultimate purpose of human history is the glorification of God.

Woe Against Inhumanity

15 Woe to him who gives drink to his neighbors, pouring it from the wine skins until they are drunk, so that he can gaze on their naked bodies!

16 You will be filled with shame instead of glory. Now it is your turn! Drink and let your nakedness be exposed! The cup of the Lord's right hand is coming around to you, and disgrace will cover your glory.

17 The violence you have done to Lebanon will overwhelm you, and your destruction of animals will terrify you. For you have shed human blood; you have destroyed lands and cities and everyone in them.

The Babylonians are here likened to a person who feigns hospitality by offering neighbors a cup of wine intending only to intoxicate and embarrass them. Just as the Babylonians enslaved and humiliated its neighboring nations, so God promises to pour out a cup of divine wrath and justice upon them. When Babylonians conquered enemy territories, they routinely destroyed every person, plant and animal. As they have done unto others, so also they will suffer the humiliation and devastation of complete defeat.

Woe Against Idolatry

18 "Of what value is an idol carved by craftsmen? Or an image that teaches lies. For the one who makes it trusts in his own creation; he makes idols that cannot speak.

19 Woe to him who says to wood, 'Come to life!' Or to lifeless stone, 'Wake up!' Can it give guidance? It is covered with gold and silver. There is no breath in it."

20 The Lord is in his holy temple. Let all the earth be silent before him.

The final woe reveals the worthlessness of Babylonian polytheistic idol worship. Trusting in idols is utterly futile because they are manufactured by human beings; they cannot teach truth because they cannot even speak. Since idols are created by people, to trust them is to trust one's own creation rather than the creator. In contrast to the dumb, mute idols of Babylon, the true and living God rules and guides world history from a throne high in the heavens. In light of the presence of God's glorious power, the whole earth should be awed into silence.

Chapter 4

Habakkuk's Prayer in Praise of Yahweh

Chapter three is Habakkuk's response to the revelation of God's sovereignty. It is not merely his own personal prayer; he intended for it to be sung in temple worship services. This is made evident in the first and final verses which provide instructions to the choir director. Habakkuk composed this hymn by weaving together the words of two ancient Hebrew epic poems that praise God for delivering Israel from Egyptian slavery and leading the newly formed nation into the promised land. *1* A prayer of Habakkuk the prophet, on Shigionoth.

Shigionoth is a musical notation signaling that the prayer is to be sung in a spirit of triumph together with instrumental accompaniment.

Prayer for Mercy

2 Lord, I have heard of your fame; I stand in awe of your deeds,

Lord. Repeat them in our day, in our time make them known; in wrath remember mercy.

The word here translated as Lord is Habakkuk's first use of the name Yahweh which is God's covenant name. Habakkuk invokes Yahweh as the covenant keeping God. He praises Yahweh for previous divine deeds of deliverance and pleads for a demonstration of divine power again by requesting that God presently show mercy even in the midst of dispensing wrath.

Yahweh's Awesome Appearance

3 God came from Teman, the Holy One from Mount Paran. His glory covered the heavens and his praise filled the earth.
4 His splendor was like the sunrise; rays flashed from his hand, where his power was hidden.

Habakkuk begins his prayer of praise by commemorating God's guidance of the nation during its sojourn from Mt. Sinai to the promised land across the Jordan River. Habakkuk depicts the theophany by which God led the armies of Israel into Canaan. The divine splendor is that which vividly reveals the otherwise invisible God. The splendor of God's glory appears as a brilliant display of light. Habakkuk may have in mind the pillar of fire by which God led Israel into the promised land. Like bright rays from the sun, God's splendor does not fully reveal but points to the center of the divine source from which it emanates.

5 Plague went before him; pestilence followed his steps. 6 He stood, and shook the earth; he looked, and made the nations tremble. The ancient mountains crumbled and the age-old hills collapsed–but God marches on forever. 7 I saw the tents of Kushan in distress, the dwellings of Midian in anguish.

Plague and pestilence are personified as part of God's entourage, presented here as God's servants of divine judgment on the Egyptians. The earthquakes, which accompanied the advance of the Israeli army, are here contemplated as acts of God that instilled fear in the hearts of Israel's enemies.

Yahweh's Power Over Nature

8 Were you angry with the rivers, Lord? Was your wrath against the streams? Did you rage against the sea when you rode your horses and your chariots to victory? *9* You uncovered your bow, you called for many arrows. *10* You split the earth with rivers; the mountains saw you and writhed. Torrents of water swept by; the deep roared and lifted its waves on high. *11* Sun and moon stood still in the heavens at the glint of your flying arrows, at the lightning of your flashing spear.

Habakkuk pictures God's wrath as directed against the waters of the Red Sea in which God drowned the Egyptians. God's righteous anger is an expression of divine judgment. Anger, wrath and rage depict God's righteous actions against all human enemies and natural obstacles that threaten to thwart God's will. Habakkuk presents God metaphorically as a conquering king, riding a chariot of fire and armed with weapons of war. And while God does not advocate war or violence, God sovereignly steers warring nations to accomplish divine justice in the world.

Yahweh's Power Over the Enemy

12 In wrath you strode through the earth and in anger you threshed the nations. *13* You came out to deliver your people, to save your anointed one. You crushed the leader of the land of wickedness. You stripped him from head to foot. *14* With his own spear you pierced his head when his warriors stormed out to scatter us, gloating as though about to devour the wretched who were in hiding. *15* You trampled the sea with your horses, churning the great waters.

Just as God demonstrated power over natural obstacles, so God displayed power over the nations that menaced Israel. God is here celebrated for delivering Israel and its leader Moses from Egyptian bondage, and for dealing defeat to the pharaoh of Egypt. God is metaphorically depicted as a heroic warrior who rescued Israel by drowning the enemy army in the Red Sea.

Habakkuk's Response

16 I heard and my heart pounded, my lips quivered at the sound; decay crept into my bones, and my legs trembled. Yet I will wait patiently for the day of calamity to come on the nation invading us.

From the earth quaking revelation of God at Sinai to the splitting of the waters of the Red Sea, God's powerful presence has been made known to the covenant community of Israel. God had granted Habakkuk a vision of the divine wrath which simultaneously destroyed the Egyptians and delivered Israel from bondage. As he contemplated God's frightful power over all natural obstacles and enemies of Israel, Habakkuk was shaken to the core of his entire being–body, blood and bones. The point of Habakkuk's poem is plain and simple: if God could destroy the oppressive pharaoh of Egypt and his armies, then God can defeat the arrogant king of Babylon and all his fierce, fighting forces. Nevertheless, Habakkuk knows that the judgment of God upon Judah is imminent and inevitable. In light of God's past acts of deliverance, Habakkuk is prepared to face the impending disaster brought on Judah by the brutal Babylonians. He takes great consolation in knowing that although God will chastise the covenant community, the cruel Babylonians will be divinely punished in due course. Moreover, Habakkuk can rest assured that God is in control of history, causing all things to work together for good. He is confident that God will show mercy to a faithful remnant, even in the midst of judgment.

17 Though the fig tree does not bud and there are no grapes on the vines, though the olive crop fails and the fields produce no food, though there are no sheep in the pen and no cattle in the stalls, *18* yet I will rejoice in the Lord, I will be joyful in God, my savior.

Habakkuk envisions and considers the land of Judah in the aftermath of the Babylonian invasion. Their cruel military conquest has destroyed every trace of life in Judah, including its flora and fauna. Despite the impending doom of devastation and desolation, Habakkuk manages to remain content and rejoice in the sufficiency of God to fulfill all his needs.

19 The Sovereign Lord is my strength; he makes my feet like the feet of a deer, he enables me to tread on the heights. For the director of music. On my stringed instruments.

Habakkuk concludes his hymn of praise, acknowledging God as the center of his life and the source of his strength. He has been raised from the depth of despair to the height of happiness. Habakkuk compares his spiritual ascent to a deer who skillfully scales a mountain and skips across its rugged terrain.

Chapter 5

Conclusion

Habakkuk teaches that God is both holy and just and deals fairly with all people everywhere. From Habakkuk's prophecy, readers are reminded and reassured of the ultimate victory of good over evil through God's control of history. When doubt and discouragement arise, believers should be like Habakkuk and take their problems directly to God in prayer. Habakkuk demonstrates that God is always readily available and directly accessible to those who reach out in prayer with their perplexities and problems. God invites conversational encounters with believers whose faith falters in the face of a world gone wrong. Even devout believers sometimes struggle with doubt about God's existence. Habakkuk emboldens believers to take their questions and doubts about God directly to God. Habakkuk models what it means to have an intimate relationship with God and promises believers a personal communion with God sufficient to dispel deep discouragement and debilitating doubt. Habakkuk further assures believers that God's holiness provides the standard for ethical behaviour which is also the basis on which God will judge the nations. Above all, Habakkuk teaches that a righteous life is lived by faith in God.

Printed in Great Britain
by Amazon

68001204R00018